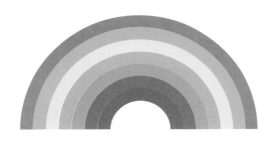

I LOVE YOU

I LOVE YOU

Compiled by Samuel Alexander

Heart and rainbow icons © mspoint/Shutterstock.com

An Hachette UK Company
www.hachette.co.uk

Summersdale Publishers Ltd
Part of Octopus Publishing Group Limited
Carmelite House,
50 Victoria Embankment
LONDON
EC4Y 0DZ
UK

www.summersdale.com

Printed and bound in the Czech Republic

ISBN: 978-1-78783-976-2

Substantial discounts on bulk quantities of Summersdale books are available to corporations, professional associations and other organizations. For details contact general enquiries: telephone: +44 (0) 1243 771107 or email: enquiries@summersdale.com.

To.........................

From......................

We are beautiful.
And I am so in love
with everything you
are and everything
you have ever been.

HALSEY

Our love is here and it's queer

IT'S ALWAYS WRONG TO HATE, BUT IT'S NEVER WRONG TO LOVE.

Lady Gaga

Loving's pretty easy.
It's letting someone
love you that's hard.

Rita Mae Brown

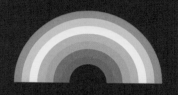

I FALL IN LOVE
EVERY TIME
I LOOK AT YOU

We deserve to
experience love fully,
equally, without shame
and without compromise.

ELLIOT PAGE

Love isn't something you find. Love is something that finds you.

LORETTA YOUNG

SPREAD LOVE, NOT HATE

The consciousness of
loving and being loved
brings a warmth and
a richness to life that
nothing else can bring.

OSCAR WILDE

We all want to love
and be loved.

MADONNA

I STILL GET BUTTERFLIES
WHEN I THINK ABOUT
SEEING YOU

Love is a human experience, not a political statement.

ANNE HATHAWAY

Will you come travel
with me? Shall we
stick by each other
as long as we live?

WALT WHITMAN

Never
apologize
for who
you love

LOVE AS HARD AS YOU CAN, AT ALL TIMES.

Sam Smith

Love is the one thing
stronger than desire and
the only proper reason
to resist temptation.

Jeanette Winterson

YOU DON'T FALL IN
LOVE WITH A GENDER
– YOU FALL IN LOVE
WITH A PERSON

I came out because
I fell in love... I was
in love with somebody,
and I wanted to scream
it from the rooftops.

GILBERT BAKER

You don't have
to be gay to be a
supporter – you just
have to be human.

DANIEL RADCLIFFE

I'LL NEVER HIDE MY LOVE FOR YOU

Love makes you
do crazy things.

TOM DALEY

Love recognizes
no barriers.

MAYA ANGELOU

LOVE ISN'T ABOUT
TWO GENDERS —
IT'S ABOUT TWO SOULS

Love is accepting people
for who they are and what
they are, regardless.

ALICIA KEYS

We are worthy
of respect,
desire and love.

JANET MOCK

All love is beautiful

WE LOVE BECAUSE IT'S THE ONLY TRUE ADVENTURE.

Nikki Giovanni

Love overcomes hate.
Love has no colour.
Love has no orientation.

Adam Lambert

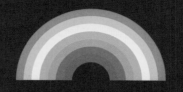

THE WORLD HAS BIGGER PROBLEMS THAN BOYS WHO KISS BOYS AND GIRLS WHO KISS GIRLS

I think there's nothing
more beautiful in the
world than falling in love.

EARTHA KITT

By doing the work to
love ourselves more,
I believe we will love
each other better.

LAVERNE COX

WE ARE
ALL HUMAN
AND WE
ALL LOVE

May we end up in a world
where everyone can
live and love equally.

TAYLOR SWIFT

I think love is love.
You can find it in
any gender.

DEMI LOVATO

FINDING YOU WAS
HARD, BUT LOVING
YOU IS EASY

I am queer.
I am into ALL humans.
I guess maybe I am
just really into love?

**DOMINIQUE
PROVOST-CHALKLEY**

Everybody should
be allowed to be who
they are, and to love
who they love.

DOLLY PARTON

Our love is all that matters

LOVE IS THE ONE THING THAT UNITES THE ENTIRE WORLD.

Eddie Izzard

You get to choose who
you love and who you
give your heart to.

Emma Watson

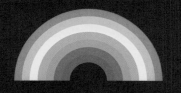

OUR LOVE IS TOO BEAUTIFUL TO HIDE IN THE CLOSET

Love will find a way
through paths where
wolves fear to prey.

LORD BYRON

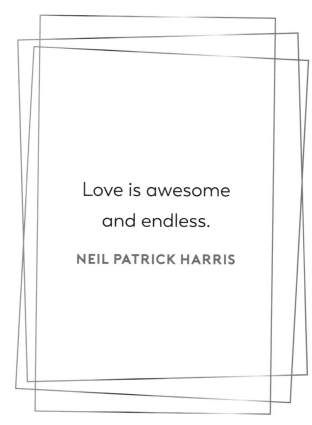

Love is awesome
and endless.

NEIL PATRICK HARRIS

LOVE
HAS
NO
GENDER

You have grown so
much to be a part
of my life that it is
empty without you.

ELEANOR ROOSEVELT

I would rather
look at you than
all the portraits
in the world.

FRANK O'HARA

LOVE IS NOT AN IDEOLOGY
AND IT NEEDS NO APOLOGY

Love takes off the masks
that we fear we cannot
live without and know we
cannot live within.

JAMES BALDWIN

I wanted to say you
looked sweeter than
a slice of ginger cake.

KIRSTY LOGAN

Our love is powerful

LOVE HAS BEEN OUR SURVIVAL.

Audre Lorde

If you truly love
something, fight
for it every day.

Keiynan Lonsdale

OUR FIRST KISS
STARTED A
REVOLUTION
IN MY HEART

Kindness always wins...
love is best served
unconditionally.

DAN LEVY

If grass can grow
through cement, love
can find you at every
time in your life.

CHER

TAKE

PRIDE

IN

LOVE

Happiness is pretty simple: someone to love, something to do, something to look forward to.

RITA MAE BROWN

I didn't want
to live a life
without love.

EDIE WINDSOR

I COULD SPEND A WHOLE DAY
WITH YOU AND STILL MISS
YOU THE MOMENT YOU LEAVE

Love has no gender –
compassion has no
religion – character
has no race.

ABHIJIT NASKAR

We're entitled to
be loved, and seek
happiness, and share
that with the people
that we care about.

**MISS MAJOR
GRIFFIN-GRACY**

Love
is love

TILL I LOVED I NEVER LIVED.

Emily Dickinson

I don't judge,
I just love.

Marlon Wayans

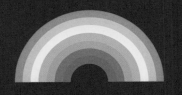

LOVE
BRILLIANTLY
AND WITHOUT
REGRET

I'm a big proponent
of all love winning and
love just being fab.

JONATHAN VAN NESS

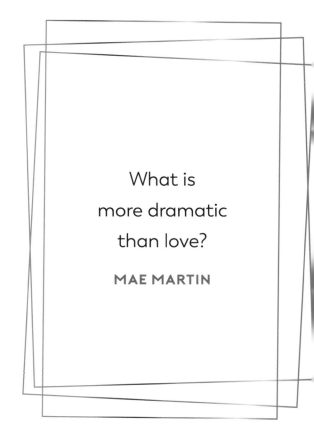

What is
more dramatic
than love?

MAE MARTIN

THANK
YOU FOR
SHARING
YOUR LOVE
WITH ME

We all have the choice
to spread love, encourage
individuality and make
a difference to others.

CHRISTINA AGUILERA

Who,
being loved,
is poor?

OSCAR WILDE

I LIKE IT WHEN YOU SMILE,
BUT I LOVE IT WHEN
I'M THE REASON

To me, our love is so
great that I feel it cannot
exist without all the
world being aware of it.

GORDON BOWSHER

Love is like music.
It knows no boundaries
and isn't exclusive
to any one gender,
sexuality, race, religion,
age or creed.

ARIANA GRANDE

YOU ARE FULL OF LOVE, AND YOU ARE LOVED.

Hayley Williams

Love weaves itself from
hundreds of threads.

David Levithan

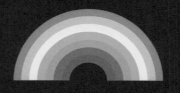

WHEN YOU REDUCE
LOVE TO BLACK AND
WHITE, YOU NEVER
SEE RAINBOWS

In case you ever
foolishly forget:
I am never not
thinking of you.

VIRGINIA WOOLF

I think romance is
anything honest.

KRISTEN STEWART

I
LOVE
OUR
LOVE

How was it possible to be afraid, when the two of them grew stronger together every day?

PATRICIA HIGHSMITH

I want nothing from love, in short, but love.

COLETTE

LIVE OPENLY AND
LOVE PROUDLY

As soon as you really understand what it means to love, you understand what it takes to become a human being.

MADONNA

You're enough,
exactly how you
are, and there's
somebody out there
who knows that.

SAMIRA WILEY

Love is
never wrong

NOW FILL THE WORLD WITH MUSIC, LOVE AND PRIDE.

Lin-Manuel Miranda

Love each other.
Period.
Love each other.
No judgment.

Sara Bareilles

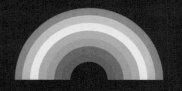

LOVE COMES IN SO
MANY COLOURS,
AND I LOVE YOU
WITH EVERY SHADE
OF MY HEART

O Heart
O Love
Everything is
suddenly turned
to gold!

ALLEN GINSBERG

Some say my loving

you is wrong, but

I love you because

it feels so right.

ANONYMOUS

LOVE IS
FOR
EVERYBODY

I love you because the entire universe conspired to help me find you.

PAULO COELHO

Love is an emotion
that has no barriers.

CÉLINE DION

♥

MY FAVOURITE PLACE
TO BE IS IN YOUR ARMS

I love you. I feel like
I can be my truest self
when I am around you.

MJ RODRIGUEZ

We all deserve
equal respect and
the right to love.

STEFAN OLSDAL

Let's celebrate our love

LOVE IS
BEAUTIFUL.

Brendon Urie

My advice to you
is never chase love –
it will find you when
you least expect it.

Elton John

IN A WORLD WITH
SO MUCH HATRED,
EVERYONE SHOULD
BE ALLOWED TO LOVE

Love shared between
two people should be
praised, not condemned.

KELLY CLARKSON

Love is the hardest
habit to break, and
the most difficult
to satisfy.

DREW BARRYMORE

LOVING YOU IS ALL I WANT TO DO

I have always
believed in love;
I've always put
my heart in love.

RuPAUL

There is no fear when you choose love.

MELISSA ETHERIDGE

WHEN YOU'RE NOT HERE,
I COUNT DOWN THE DAYS
UNTIL I CAN SEE YOU AGAIN

I miss you even more than
I could have believed;
and I was prepared to
miss you a good deal.

VITA SACKVILLE-WEST

Accept no one's
definition of your life –
define yourself.

HARVEY FIERSTEIN

I smile
whenever
I think of
your face

YOU HAVE NO IDEA HOW STRONG MY LOVE IS!

Elizabeth Gilbert

Love yourself
first and everything
else falls in line.

Lucille Ball

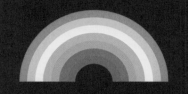

THE BEST DAYS OF MY LIFE ARE THE ONES I SPEND WITH YOU

When I fell in love,
all the shame and guilt
I carried with me for years
suddenly vanished.

GILBERT BAKER

I fall in love
with girls and guys.
I can't help it.

AUBREY PLAZA

YOU
FILL MY
WORLD
WITH
COLOUR

The only
queer people are
those who don't
love anybody.

RITA MAE BROWN

I'm possessed
by love – but isn't
everybody?

FREDDIE MERCURY

LOVE IS THE SOLUTION, NEVER THE PROBLEM

When you love yourself,
that's when you're
most beautiful.

ZOË KRAVITZ

Love makes your
soul crawl out from
its hiding place.

ZORA NEALE HURSTON

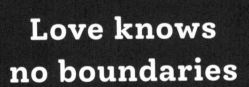

Love knows
no boundaries

I AM
BI YOUR
SIDE.
ALL WAYS.

Jason Mraz

You are my heart, my life,
my entire existence.

Julie Kagawa

WHEN I'M WITH YOU, THE WHOLE WORLD STOPS

We want to be
loved and seen and
held fully as who
we fully are.

JANET MOCK

If you find someone
you love in your life,
then hang on to
that love.

**DIANA,
PRINCESS OF WALES**

LOVE
HAS
NO
LABELS

The only beautiful eyes
are those that look at
you with tenderness.

COCO CHANEL

We vibrate
on the same
frequency.

TESSA THOMPSON

LET YOURSELF
LOVE WHO YOU LOVE

Every memory of your
face, every cadence of
your voice is joy whereon
I shall feed hungrily in
these coming months.

MARGARET MEAD

In all the world
there is no heart
for me like yours.

MAYA ANGELOU

My love
for you has
no limits

LOVE IS FRIENDSHIP SET TO MUSIC.

Jackson Pollock

I believe much more
in love and heart.

Lea T

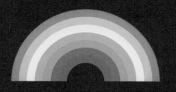

LIFE IS TOO
SHORT TO SPEND
IT WITHOUT YOU

Never forget,
dear one, how deeply
I have loved you
all these years.

RACHEL CARSON

Love shall be our
token; love be yours
and love be mine.

CHRISTINA ROSSETTI

YOU
ARE
ALWAYS
IN MY
HEART

I've always said since I was younger, I fall in love with a soul rather than a gender.

ANGIE KENT

We can climb
mountains
with self-love.

SAMIRA WILEY

I LOVE YOU FOR
EVERYTHING YOU ARE

When you love someone,
all your saved-up wishes
start coming out.

ELIZABETH BOWEN

I can live without
money, but I cannot
live without love.

JUDY GARLAND

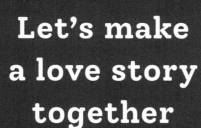

Let's make a love story together

IT MUST BE UNDERSTOOD THAT LOVE COMES FIRST.

Stephen Fry

My love is not measured
in reciprocity. That's not
the way I learned love.

Indya Moore

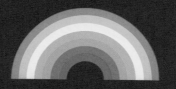

EVERYONE
DESERVES TO LOVE
AND BE LOVED

To be brave is to love
someone unconditionally,
without expecting
anything in return.

MADONNA

If you are not too
long, I will wait here
for you all my life.

OSCAR WILDE

LIVE
BOLDLY
AND
LOVE
FIERCELY

Life is full of choices.
Loving you isn't
one of them –
I have no control
over that.

ANONYMOUS

If it's love, it's love...
That's all that matters.

KYLIE MINOGUE

Wouldn't it be wonderful
if all our letters could be
published in the future in
a more enlightened time.
Then all the world could see
how in love we are.

GORDON BOWSHER

I LOVE YOU

Have you enjoyed this book? If so, find us on Facebook at **Summersdale Publishers**, on Twitter at **@Summersdale** and on Instagram at **@summersdalebooks** and get in touch. We'd love to hear from you!

www.summersdale.com